For my _Dear_ _Mother_
I love you!
Loraine

Dear Mom

By Shirley Hepton

Illustrated by Victoria

PEANUT BUTTER PUBLISHING
SEATTLE, WASHINGTON

ISBN 0-89716-374-5
Peanut Butter Publishing
200 Second Avenue West
Seattle, Washington 98119

Cover Design: Graphiti Associates
Editor & Book Designer: Nancy M. Pascoe

Dedicated to my mother, Olga

In Remembrance of

Glenola Hollister McCreery — Procastination
Harold Wayne (Hal) Hollister — The Comforter
Craig Albert Hollister — Afterglow
&
Orman Laben Miller
July 13, 1893 - April 3, 1986

Mr. Miller, country lawyer and poet of Pottawatomie
County, Kansas, was the younger brother of Olga Mae
Schoeffer, for whom this book was written.
Included from his works are:
I Shall Not See This Day Again
Farmer's Wife
Ballad of The Old Time Country Dance

Contents

Preface

While not all of the poems in this book are either to or about my mother, they are all a reflection of her influence, of the principles and standards that were hers, and of her firm belief that "We are placed on earth with certain talents and capabilities and it is up to each to use them as best we can. If we do, there is a power greater than any of us that will place opportunity in our way."

Dear Mom is her book.

Introduction

I often thought it a tragedy of placement. Born to younger children of two large families, I knew little of the people who shaped the two who would then shape me.

But the tragedy fades as the hues of life and death color a path which leads me closer to parents and grandparents who leave plenty behind to know.

The tales seem to expand with each telling — half-filled stomachs, seven mile walks to a one-room school-house, icy nights and oranges that brought smiles on Christmas morning. There were hand-me-downs and newspapered soles; a horse named Lady and a step-father Henry; chores a natural part of every day and a resilient woman at the center of it all.

She was "Mom" to everyone, her title rarely questioned. Though my years with her were few, the memories are clear. I, with my brother and two sisters, had come to know three different houses where she lived. She had many, each filled with the things that kept her busy.

I recall the tools and crafts of quilting, crochet, and embroidery; flowers which colored many rooms; kitchens decorated with bright fruits and vegetables in canning jars; stacks of magazines piled on the table and the smell of books shelved nearby.

Outside, abundant gardens enticed our curious minds. They offered hours of adventure and numerous lessons in the magic of cultivation.

I often confused Mom's seasoned strength and independence with a cold sternness. She was a woman hardened by life with a character easily likened to stubbornness. Yet, it was never enough to frighten me, because I knew she loved us. And over the years I am continually reminded of that love and of the person she became.

She was in gardens of my youth and now in gardens of my own. Her music rests on the piano waiting to be played. Her lemon meringue pie often completes a holiday meal.

I feel her endless appetite for information and interest in politics, which Dad has passed to me. I know her values of honesty, hard work, and self-reliance. Indeed, her willful ways are as familiar.

In tribute to Mom, her life echoes across these pages. And in honor of all mothers, these words and illustrations reflect the power and the importance of what we leave behind for others to know.

— Corinne Hollister, February 1991

Teen Years

What don't I have
That I should have
Or what is wrong with him
My qualities are evident
As the spiney chestnut's shell.

I am intelligent and talented
I'm lovely
Each spine upon the chestnut
Speaks for me
Yet I'm a buddy—I'm a pal
I am asked to meet him
In baseball practice clothes
When I long to be beheld
In trailing dress and earrings
And something number five.

Why can't he see me as I am
My parts aren't crossed or bowed
I am not humped or banjo-eyed
My braces are long gone
Is he lacking in perception
Or is there something wrong with me?

In the Beginning

From high upon the windswept boulders
Of the city by the bay
I watched
As footprints that had led me there
Were swiftly washed away
I was come from nowhere—going nowhere
With the you so soon to be
And the hope that you'd be patterned
With my feeling for the sea.

Always with me
Unborn child
Sharing in my visions
And my dreams
Taking what I have to give
And growing....

I am earthbound
Solid as the boulders on the beach
You are fanciful and free
Moving with abandon
Forming your own tributary
From the streambed of my life
Your movements as restless as the sea.

I am absolute—you infinity
Free soon to embrace a world
Of possibles
To dip into the universe
And paint a better world
With your life.

Until then you are of me
A captive of my world
As I walk with you beside the sea
While you are still asleep.

Unity

Have I told you
That I love the way you stand so tall
And reach so wide
And that your whole life is with you
Not forgotten in some twisty shady lane
That you have passed
Nor sectioned into past and present
But kept as one
Together
In what you are?

Olga

Deltas deep and rich and wide
Appeared as wastelands
As they slid beneath her chin
Cradling the years of their creation,
Blank mirrored eyes looked crossly back
Not knowing who was pictured there.

The once-blue-laughing eyes were gray
Though clear, still looking both directions
She turned from what appeared of her
And chose a different time to be.

With swinging hair that caught the sun
Eyes early summer blue,
Feet firm rooted in a land
Of forests, streams and violets,
A land of sweet Glen Millers
In a room of rhythmed feet
A tiny waist
A guiding arm
A riccocheting skirt
She was earth and air and happiness
A river flowing free.

But swift she went from twig to oak
From queen to daily drone
The tiny waist was pushed and pulled
Its body fed the world
She looked around to find herself
But she had disappeared.

Children and their children
Kept pushing her along
Through hustling years
The deltas spread
Inside she was unchanged
What was of her was still of her
She found herself again.

"Grandma's smiling," someone said
And grandma was,
Deep rooted still within the earth
With shining hair
And summer eyes.

JAYLENE DISCOVERING NATURE AND
ALL THE WONDERS IT HOLDS FOR A CHILD

Diminished

When I was an unlearned child
I ran and screamed into the wind
And tried for things beyond
My ability to do.

Years slid by
I went to school
To learn the things society
Determined I must know.

I took the tests of aptitude
And though I'm bored by what I do
I function well within the niche
That proper tests have brought me to.

No longer do I fly the wind
Or try for things I cannot do.

Lost

I always liked eyes cool and clear
But his were secret.

They hid behind a blue-gray sea
Revealing nothing.

I had to know what was beyond
That opaque screen.

There were no road signs
I misjudged and tumbled in.

Did I want out? I said I did
But doubtfully.

To show sincerity I strived
But languidly.

Will power and my common sense
Of which I'm proud

Helped bring me back and plant my feet
On solid ground

Till happy-sad and empty-free
I turned around

To look my last on quiet sea
And when I did

Most happily
Sad-empty-free abandoned me.

Forsaken

The day just ran away
And left me there
And though I said
I didn't care
I knew I really did.

Shadows

Sometimes I can't remember
What you look like,
You merge with Everyman
Like Gene Kelly into Fred Astaire.
At times I cannot separate
The beauty of those two
And it really doesn't matter,
The feeling that remains from seeing them
Can change a life
The same as you.

Reflections

When I drove in from the lake today
I was upset about the pump
That doesn't work
And trees that grow across the chimney
So that fires can't light the cabin
After dark
And then I thought of you
Of your dark brown eyes and hair
And lovely skin.

I thought of how the day
Is brighter when you smile
And of how you make the world
A fascinating place
In which to be.

I thought of how you dance
While others plod through life
And I was not concerned
About the pump that doesn't work
Or of trees
That grow across the chimney
So that fires
Can't light the cabin after dark.

I Shall Not See This Day Again

I shall not see this day again
Out of the void it crept at dawn
A gift not bought with prayer or price
Though loath to see it die at night
Hope will not stay its fated flight

I was a pauper when it came
A bankrupt as it fades away
Though faltered I on yesterday
Or like an arrant coward
Flee tomorrow from some test supreme
Yet none may say that I have failed
If I be kind and true today.

by Orman L. Miller

True Love

He named all the bugs in the basement
He loved them he said with delight,
He would play with them
All through the daytime
He would stay with them
All through the night.

But he left them and now they are lonely
They feel his affection was false
They say "Was his love really true love
When across half the world he could waltz?"

They say that he said that he loved them
But ask "Did he really
When he is out walking
In Vietnam freely
And we are left lonely
And cold in the dark?"

He walked up the stairs and he left them
Left Maria and Christian and Marc
After promising them a bug heaven
In the high rising green of Cliff Park.

Since he went away they are sad
They are blue
A great many vices they madly pursue
Green bugs chase brown bugs
They gorge and they drink
They hide in dark corners
And breed in the sink
And the basement is wet with their tears.

Maria cried longest
She loved him the most
She lingers
Entrapped in an aura of hope
With the passing of time
She's become but a skin
Yet her love fills the basement
And waits there for him.

Flower Girl

Red and white and blue
The students of Kent State
Moved almost casually
Toward the line of National Guardsmen
With flowers and a sureness
That Vietnam was wrong.

Allison stepped forward
With daisies for the guns
But Goliath was in David's shoes
And flowers were not used
Rifles leveled
Triggers pulled
Allison left the land of the free
Without farewell.

The guardsmen
"Fine human beings,
Entitled to the gratitude
Of all in this free land,"
Felt Red and White and Blue
As daisy petals drifted
And the pages of history books
Turned red.

Bryant's God?

How not lost, the wanderer
Whose search for someone not avail
And Who allowing depths of Hell
Guides winging of the wandered quail?

Who holds taut the thread of life
That man slip smooth from end to end
What Eye all-seeing shares the pain
Of trials that wrack the human frame?

Whose punishments so misbegot
For crimes undone or long forgot
Who is it tends the seeds of weeds
That bear fruit for the tiny tot?

Justice

H is eyes were kind
Benevolent and good
From years of practice
As he announced that
Right and wrong
Were really wrong and right
And that good and bad
Could each be made into the other
Or be differently defined
(Depending on the viewpoint
And where the silver lay.)

The dockets in his court
Were cleared
The cases settled,
Decided more by politics
And golf and luncheon dates
Than fact or evidence.

Yet
How like a priest he looked
In his black robes
Dispensing days in court
To all the supplicants.

A New Beginning

$\mathcal{D}$ isembodied hours go by
One after one
I count them
And the raindrops, birds and bees
The flow of rivers to the seas
Stand in windswept wheat grown high
And yet lie sleepless.

Soon now the birds' bright melodies
I'll hear
Sweet music from the maple trees
The hound's first lonely waking cry
Will come to me.

Thus last night and other nights I lay
While ashes of a burned out night
Were giving birth to day.

The Healer

I'd come for tests
Though my concern was not for these
But for the fact
That man is mostly in his mind
And I was not in mine.

I was down
My world was wrong
I sat and waited while a throng
Of patients
Mostly young
Circled through a growing line.

Surrounded and depressed
By the ebb and flow of life
And the endless cavalcade
Of clumsy tight-walled pregnancy
Which anxiously awaited giving birth
To link the two
I pressed back tight
Against the multiplying ugliness
And knew I must escape.

The door was close
And just beyond
The anonymity of vacant hallway
But no spirit moved to save me.

A girl in lavender and purple
Entombed in her expectancy
Smiled at me with sympathy
But I just looked away
Disjunct
Counted all the feet in pairs
Before the armied legs of chairs
Waited for my skull to crack
And scatter what was left of me
Dull gray
Across the floor.

My name was called
It was in your voice
And in your eyes
That I was not a number
You remembered me.

And I remember now
Not the carpet's color
Although
I must have memorized each thread
But the girl in lavender
More wholly pregnant
Than any I had ever seen
Clumsy, yes, but soft and round
Lovely
Dark hair parted
Pulled back smooth
Waiting for her child.

She looked up as I was leaving
And she smiled
This time so did I.

No Yardstick

He loves me well
He told me so
He also said he well loves Joe
John, Bob and Henry, Jim and Paul
No weed among them
Best friends all.

At first I thought him really great
Till asked to share my space with Kate
And Jenny, Joan and all the rest
He's ever known, roses all
And all of whom he loves the best.

I think that I will just move on
And find a dandelioned lawn.

Procrastination

She was leaving
My younger sister
Transported on a bed of pain
There was no bridge that I could walk
To stay her flight.

I sent a gift "The Sounds of Silence"
And too late did I hear silence
As it would come to her
I started something better
A poem of our younger days.

She would often ask about it
This poem by a poet who wasn't one
I told of other things
For this special gift
With dew still holding in the bud
Should grow as we had grown
And be presented tall and proud
Not be dribbled in a
Scattering of petals.

I worked on it between all other things
I thought I had to do (Oh send it)
But I did not work on it
As often or as hard
Or as consistently
As I now know I needed to
Because of this she still asks
About the poem (Send it please)

I worked on but easily
I had no sense of urgency
(Please send it now)
Day followed day and I revised
Until I found no more to do
It was a jewel
I took it to the mailbox
And dropped it into darkness.

Nineteen is Younger than I Thought

When I was cleaning out your room
I came across some things
That made me smile
And some that hurt,
Weird mobiles made of colored wire
And a letter that you left
To say goodbye.

I searched for weeks and months
And almost years
In every street and alleyway,
Then when the world
Was turning white
The summer cabin came to me.

There I found a note
Addressed to no one
Saying that you didn't mind
The loneliness and cold
But that the empty windows after dark
Were fearsome.

Shining clean beside the door
Were an unused litter box
And an empty hamster cage
Mute evidence
That now you were alone.

Before I left
I left a note
And for weeks
The table asked the ceiling
To come home.

My own nineteen is too far gone
For me to know just where to turn
And bats and mice and monkey men
Are messing up my head
Because you're gone and time is gone
And these are years of yours
That I will never know.

Dear Mom

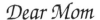

I was digging in the soft warm earth today
To make a bed for my nasturtiums
The almost setting sun was warm
Against my back
And a single gull
Low-swinging
Split the evening with its loneliness
But mostly it was quiet
And I found myself pulled backwards
Through all the building blocks of years
That formed your life
While you were forming ours.

I am afraid that none of us
Have ever told how much we've loved you
Or of our joy
That our communal character is good
And is in keeping with the standards
That you gave us
As you managed to maintain life—
Yours and ours—
When all that lay ahead was one more day.

We know the hardship
And the loneliness and hurt
That formed the backbone
Of all that you became
Yet we are rich in memories
Of home-made candy Easter eggs
Fluorescent pink and white and brown
Of multicolored birthday cakes
Christmas trees of two-by-fours
Drilled and filled with boughs
Of sweet ground-cedar
Montana rocks and rattlesnakes
Coulees deep and crescent-shaped and green
Scattered by a careless hand
Across the drying prairie
And haystacks silvered by the moon
Where we could play at night
Halfway between the coyote's cry
And the window where the oil lamp was lit.

Interwoven with our closeness
Was the freedom to roam and learn at will
To touch the sky and hold the wind
And taste the raindrops as they fell
Across the seeds you brought to life
Year after year.
As we grew and traveled westward from Montana
Across each new horizon a golden image spilled
Encircling the plants we needed for survival
Were your flowers
With always as a signature nasturtiums.

Memory tells me nothing
Of the sometimes cold and hunger
But holds unending
To that shining thread of gold.

Afterglow

Gravity brought down the sun
The day was dark
The candle done
A branch had left the tree.

Those left
Can't file away the pain
Cannot grieve once
And not again.

Yet the weeping willow is aware
That all must go.
He went
With bloom still seeking
Through the leaves
No sadness
From the burgeoning years
No gray, no weight to bear
No tears—

Now soft through undulating leaves
Cresting with the morning sun
Quiet in the evening breeze
His song is ever sung.

Lady of the Forest

There stands a tree
Full breasted
Solid as the earth from which it springs
Yet separate,
Narrowing to pierce the earth
Then spreading forth with equal girth below,
Both ends held captive by the
Rough-hewn dumbbell grip of trunk
That binds the two together.

Mid-trunk two hands are firmly clasped
The heart
The breath
And they are wed
A bride
A lover dancing free
A joyous carefree child
Dancing in the blackened night
Holding high a rain-drenched face
To rising wind and flashing light
Flinging, writhing through the storm
In total self-abandonment.

The trunk responds
And roots hold fast
Sweet ballast for the surging rite.

Earth moves slowly
Daylight comes
Slender undulating leaves
Move softly on the air
Telling to the trunk below
"The man, the boy
Still tented here
Will always be too young to know
The life that is a tree.

Growing Up

I walked along the lakeshore
With my brother and my sister
Wondering should I be happy
That our relationship
Is filled with love and laughter?
Or should I more rightly feel sad
To not be walking with someone
Who would turn me into stardust.

Someone perhaps
Who would flatter me
Beyond all common sense
Who would himself pretend to be
A thing much greater
Than fact would indicate
As truth
And thus would open up the door
For my pretense
A carbon copy of what he had begun
So that each of us
Would represent perfection.

I turned my back upon the image
To adjust my stride back to my siblings
But soon I do believe
I will turn the other way
And create a split
To faintly parallel
The San Andreas Fault.

I know that it will hurt
When our world breaks apart
But each of us in turn
Will bear the pain.

Blueprint

I just got home
From my last day at work
To find my universe
With nothing but tag-ends,
I think it is because
I will no longer have a desk
That faces half away from you
So that I see you
Sometimes with my eyes
And sometimes from behind them.

I will no longer hear your voice
As an obbligato to the typing
And know that you've said something
Probably ridiculous
To bring a ray of light
Into the room.

I don't have to wonder what it is
That makes you different
For you are highly moral
And highly ethical,
You believe in your beliefs
And do not sway.

Your splendid sense of humor
Serves you well
You catch the fun in things
But do not laugh when fun is gone
And crudeness blunders in.

You've helped to make my world go round
With a semblance of good order
And you've become the blueprint
Of a friend.

Home

*W*hat happened to the kitchen sink
The mirror in the dining room
The bathroom light switch
And the window of the car—
The right-hand front—
Which I could see through yesterday
Before the new-created many branching
Opaque delta
That appears to have been managed
From within?
The hammers sledges rocks or clubs
That must have wrought the havoc
Are scarcely instruments of peace and quiet.

The switch was pulverized so fine
The rug sucked in its powder,
There must have been some noise somewhere
In all these many years
Or was it elves that crunched the sink
And squared the oblong mirror?
Did fairies cart away the leavings
Put away the tools?

Catastrophes aren't silent
Whenever I'm around
I can't believe they always are for you,
Oh please! Come on and tell me
My sanity will leave me
If you leave me in this fog,
It won't be held above your head
I won't threaten, be upset
I'll not even ask about the car's
Bagged-down headliner
That rests upon my shoulders
Like accumulated laundry
When I drive,

I'll believe without the telling
That it was caused by normal wear and tear
But please explain the rest
So that my mind won't slip this way
The truth and we'll forget, I promise
Only save my sanity.

"Grades came," said Jon, "And inner man
required relief from outer activated shell,
So when the hammer sprang to hand
I sacrificed for psyche's sake."
"I did the window" Gina said,
"I leaned back sideways on the seat
And kicked and kicked until it bowed
And formed into an opaque delta,
If I didn't would I know that the delta
Had been formed?"
Julie poked her pigtails in
"Whatever's left I did," she said
"I hope you rilly think it too
Cause else I'd be the only one
That's living here that's perfect."

I lost my mind
It lay in shattered crystal drifts
Across the floor
And no one heard the crash
Except for me.

Emancipation

I cried out for a lifeline
You pushed me back and said
That your regard would be much greater
Should I take care of myself.

When drowning
One must learn
I did—and now that I can swim
We both are free of many things
We never knew we we wanted to be free of.

Awakening

It's six o'clock
Before that came five and four
And they came after two-fifteen
When we last saw each other.

It is light enough outside
To see the fat leaf-buds
That tip the branches
Of the chestnut tree
Yet everything is dark.
The bits and pieces
Of a million years
Of happiness
Have slipped away
And left me coldly wrapped
In pride or selfrespect
Or whatever else
That thing of self is called.

I promised to look after you
Here is my protection:
I give you back
To where I took you from
The slate is clean
And you are free
I cannot be your part-time
Cinderella.

The Professor

He summoned us from idle fields
Kissed by the gentle autumn breeze
To introduce us to the gulping
And the spewing
Of messages and morals
And their mechanized assembly
As the way and means to pattern
And to rule
According to accepted form
For classic literature
So that we could open all our
Tender-budded rare exotic blooms.

We climbed the ladder of his course
Convention
Rhythm
Sentiment
And recognized the gulp and spew as life
Raw and earthy, unabridged
Persona
Masculine and feminine
Decorum
Figure
Foot
Folk
Extended figure

Couplet
Form (both fixed and free)
Response and action—rising—falling
Climax
Then politically
We touched upon convention
Understatement
Overstatement
Ambiguity
Ironic royal monologue
Burlesque
Hyperbole.

We learned and then we took in hand
Our lovely
New created
Rare
Exotic blooms.
Metaphors beat powerful wings
Across the printed page
While symbols quickly hitched themselves
To our ascending star
And similes moved swift and true
Like wild deer like the death of time
With rhyme schemes intertwining
Into a pulsing pantomime.

All that is past
We learned it all
Now our immortal words
Are everywhere flown smooth and precious
Rising
Falling
Softly firm they are
And ripe
Priceless children of a fine-edged brain
With lilt
Verve
Wisdom
Wit and freshness
Tired fixedness set free
Selected words
Bright honed and polished
Syntaxed smoothly page on page
Tight-wound buds now richly open
Ah, what loveliness in bloom.

Yet he who urged the budlets open
Watched the blooms burst forth in hope
Is caught in time beneath our scope.

While we have reached the top-most rung
He is tight-wedged far below
The time has come for him to learn
How literate we have become
If he's to criticize the bloom
He must acknowledge that it is.
He must discover us
And now
Now quickly ere the muse be fled
Our margins must be splashed in red.

He must be frank
There's room
We've left the borders wide
Dispense the truth
But tactfully
Albeit with sincerity
We are no children to be fooled
Or satisfied with empty praise.

With harvest of the purest gold
A tip-toe world that need be told
He watched the lovely blossoms fade,
At lowest ebb assigned a grade.

The Puzzle

You said I was the sun the moon
The stars to you,
Then asked that I stand
In the shadows
While you took inventory
Of your estranged wife
Your married children
And your silver
So that you could best decide
What future would be ours
But you stammered on the pronoun.

For me the choice was made
I didn't feel that I could be
The shredded nuts
To top your chocolate Sundays
Or the extra pinch of salt
That might enhance the flavor
Of your other days.

Yet when I turned east
While you continued west
You cried
And said that I was most unfair
To you
And to something you referred to
As your love.

Homestead Revisited

I crossed the Clarksfork River
And angled downward into Noxon
Which came and went
Like the turning of a page.

The school of dark red brick
Which housed grades one to twelve
Back when my father taught
Was gone
Replaced by one too big and jangling new
For the town that eased away from it,
The houses were off balance
Awry with time
Caught in slow slow motion
On their way back to the land.

I drove past cardboard windows
And yards upholstered in debris
From overturned and overlooked
Trash cans
And in the early February dusk
Found again the road that leads
To Pilgrim Creek.

The mile or so
(To me it had been seven)
Eased quickly by
Until I recognized the gate
Although it sagged much lower
On its hinges
And the two familiar tamaracks
Where years before
Minute and mute
I'd stared upward
Past thin spiney branches
To behold my first airplane,
Now black and naked
They stood watch beside the house
And for an instant my throat closed
With the thought that I was home,

Though thirty years or more lay dead
Since my last ringing of the bell
The same dull globe above the door re-lit
To slant its tired eye
Along the weathered old lap-siding.

The doorknob rattled in its slot
Unsure
As though a child's hand had grasped it.
I turned before the door could open
And re-crossed the yard
A moon-relief map in the dimming light
Stretching gray and pock-marked
With the crusty tags of winter's end.

As my wheels crunched beneath the tamaracks
I hit high beam
Caught the lusty green Montana forest
Midway between its trunk and tip
And headed home.

Basket of Daisies

Youth has something shining
That age has long forgot
It does not chip away
At another's character
It asks nothing of its guardian
But that the guardian be there.

When you were on your way
From childhood
I tried to mold you
To hitch you to a moonbeam
That you might glow more brightly
I knew so well that perfection
Was the only goal
That I took apart each one
Of your endeavors
That it be polished
And given greater shine.

I forgot that music was your love
Not mine
And when you went from first
To second chair
I feared aloud
That you would not succeed
At anything.

You grew and persevered
Until today
Your music spills like daisies
From a basket
Across a hungry earth—
And I am standing tall
To walk with you.

Edge of Love

You came to me with only want,
Sweet want once decked in love's array,
Come all alone 'twas easy killed
I laughed and watched it slip away.

Did it hurt you when I laughed?
Or could you see that I was crying?
The almost-edge of love was there
And close was I again to dying.

If eye for eye can satisfy
Then jubilate, this is your day
For I was part of everything
That as I laughed just slipped away.

Can't We Try Again?

I stopped last night beside the house
At Sixth and Adams
And stood for some time in the shadow
Of the trees
Not knowing which was your apartment
Wondering how you are
If you are happy
Or at least content,
I was almost leaving
When a light went on upstairs
You were framed in the window
Your red-blond hair lit like a halo.

You were holding
Some recent extravagant invention
An early bi-plane I believe
Made of balsa wood and nylons
That no longer could be used
For their true purpose.

You wore no shirt
And while I could not see you well
You seemed much thinner
Although it could have been the angle
Of my imagination.

I wished that things were different
That I could stop and talk to you
Say that you are young
And I am sorry
That as your mother
I would wage a truce
But the light went out
And you were gone.

In the blackened world
As I headed home
The thinness of your body
Followed me.

Farmer's Wife

Her years were marked by yellowing of teeth
And fading of her smile. Like a waning moon
Her shoulders lower drooped from day to day,
In her monotonous round of diapers and dishes,
Useless gabble about taxes and lowering prices.

It was the year she lost her last front teeth,
And in that shortened span between the earth's
White shroud and resurrection of the grass,
When life's brief candles burn with flickering
Of flame. Like flies at frost time
In the fall, children began to die.
Great panic reigned and men and women were
A-feared to go unto their neighbors' aid.
Her second child fell ill, and no one came.
It gasped and choked and slowly died.
Still no one came
Though some one, kind, came quietly at night and left
A little bunch of pansies on the porch.

With unplaned boards her husband made
A hungering box which she then line with what
Was left of her silk wedding dress, the whole
Anointed she with tears. With none to lift
With sympathy the load, they gave it to the earth
There in the yard, and marked with but
A marble slab she took from off the bureau top.

Lonely, harassed by drought and worn by toil
Not seeing people weeks and months on end
This tired woman lost her mind
She sat for days there in her chair and gazed
In empty space
She would not eat and none
Could rouse her from her lethargy
One windy day in March when swirling dust
From plowed fields had blotted out the sun
Strangers came into that kitchen
Whose only window failed to light
The gloom of her who'd labored there
And at the table with its cloth of checkered red
Like blooming cacti on the desert drab
They sat and talked and marked on paper sheets
Bewildered and amazed her husband said
"I just can't understand how she could get this way
She's lived a quiet life
With nothing to disturb her here
She's hardly been outside the kitchen
For nigh on twenty years."

by Orman L. Miller

The Comforter

He died
With half his life behind
And half still stretching out ahead,
Yet left as he had lived
With grace
So that those who mourned
Were blessed
With an awareness
Of his sympathy and understanding
Of their predicament in losing him.

Keeping the Watch

Outside on the deck
Were some socks Michael left,
They neither were pretty nor clean
But dated from days
That too soon were gone
When doors still were open
And minds yet unclosed,
They were friendship
And sunshine and music and joy
Tossed in a box filled with
Old cola bottles
Some chips and a few rusty nails.

They stared at me balefully
Wondering I guess
"Will she wash us or throw us away?"
At first I thought
"Bury them out in the yard,
Just tenderly lay them to rest"
But I feared they'd take root
Push upward and grow
And trample the earth with their vigor.

Time passed me by as I tried to decide
In my sleep they were walking the earth
They laughed without end
Without any mirth
Mindless and soulless they stalked me,
Legless and shoeless
Relentless they marched
Increasing in number and size
In madness they ran
Becoming more mad
Shouting and laughing in glee
They passed up gazelles
And Hermes' winged heel
Soon they'd be trampling me.

I screamed out in horror
A sound never heard
It swelled in the silence
And burst in my throat
As I huddled entombed
In my terror and sweat
I promised the socks
I would save them.

I washed them and dried them
And folded and pressed them
Wrapped them in tissue
Enclosed in a box
Solemnly promised to love
And protect them
Thus the vigil for Michael
Was joined by his socks.

Recycled

I cried last night for the death of a friend
But really the friend hadn't died
He had just turned his back
And had walked away
With newer hands reaching
Why should he stay?
He must search his own search
For his "happiness day"
If somewhere is sunshine
Why walk in the gray?

New loves will come
Hands extended, smiles gay
To carbon the ones
That he's turned away.

I stand all alone
At the head of a grave
And watch the slow dirt sifting in
Feeling nothing at all
As the mound grows high
But the rightness of burying
Things that die.

Golden Standard

Love-blinded to a wounded world
Step by step his dream he planned
Seldom seen by light of day
This was a dedicated man.

Knew not of filth-congested breathing
Bank notes clutched to fevered chest
Of all good things his world embraced
Money in the bank was best.

Whether rain or snow or summer
Shafted light brought forth his day
Before each dark, begot begot
Greed ignored advancing gray.

Longevity he'd wed to wealth
Unite to him his golden joy
Confident he'd live to relish
Love yet unclaimed, this aged boy.

Poor withered one he could not die
Who had not yet begun to live
Time simply made him cease to be
Bequeathed his bride to relatives.

Orbit

When the earth has turned
From green to gold
When all the leaves have fallen
And snows lay heavy on the branch
Then once more green
And gold and white
Where will you be?

Autocrat

I forgot his birth
A single day
And he set out
To make me pay
My treachery at my feet he laid
Until he felt I'd fully paid.

Then he wandered back to me
To ask for an apology
So that he could set me free
From guilt he had bequeathed to me.

I told him he could go to hell
That we would both
Be served quite well
Should he agree to this.

He said he didn't find this right
Asked that I join his wingless flight
To keep love on an even keel
Whether or not it was for real.

Love? I said
What is this thing
That you can hide away
And then bring back
For your inspection and approval
Without regard for what I feel?

He didn't understand my words
Tossed them out like wheyless curds
Said I now was in good standing
We could on with our planning
Why was I complaining?

For thirty days he'd punished me
Then had wandered back to see
If our relationship I'd missed
I looked at him but saw instead
A flaming, roiling, writhing red
I can't remember what I said.

Now everything is peace and quiet
I am myself and all alone
The time might come
Some soft warm night
When I will think I want him still
I trust that common sense will stop me
Tell me I have had my fill.

A Small Branch of the Tree

I became a part of history
The day my aunt died
And I was left to manage
Whatever grief I may have felt
While adults all clung together
Each to help another with his suffering
Except for my mother
Who in pain had pulled inside herself
And closed the door.

I paced along the library shelves
North to south and east to west
Walking slowly
Fingers trailing
Along the cramped spines of the books
Dipping in and out of history
I went like Alice through the looking glass
Into another world
And I became a book
My history wrapped within me
Like all the other volumes
Standing at attention
Each a little bit suspicious of the others
Jealous of the past and future
The happiness and pain
Clutched tight between each one's
Protecting cover.

It was quiet
A place for solving problems
And meditating on the cycled life of man,
Here I would not think about my aunt
Whose hair was long and swinging
When the slightest breeze
Would catch it up
And whose eyes turned upward just a little
When she smiled.

I would not even think about her hands
That were so pretty
But for the little finger
That overlapped the others
Instead I thought of Shakespeare,
My fingers traveling forward
And of Mark Twain
I loved him for his wondrous humor
And I loved my aunt
Who was here just yesterday.
I loved the tiny waist
That looked so pretty
Getting tanned upon the beach.
Had I ever told her?

I tried to think of Henry James
But he wouldn't come to me
Because my aunt had died
And my mother had gone inside
And closed the door.

Triangle

High above the smooth-flowed waters of her life
She stands
Like Liberty
Upon a pedestal of gold or silver
A goddess
Paragon of all the worthy virtues
Serene and far removed
From all such mundane things as chicken pox
And shedding dogs and cats
And grocery bills.

She does not stoop to competition
But graciously receives
The gifts of reverence
Heaped at her feet
She dreams down across her subjects
And she shines.

From far below I realize
That only fools would come against
So formidable a queen.

I stand alone
Feet mired in the clay of kids
And cats and leaking roofs
And bills that never quite get paid
Listening to reflected joyous strains
"Long live the Queen."

Rewards

I found within my treasure chest
Gems I knew not I possessed
Pure gold from battles waged and won
Proud songs of you all left unsung.

They tell a tale of when you asked
That I let down your glen-plaid slacks
For an athletic meeting
I didn't know you well enough
To know that you had lettered
And so I didn't lengthen them
I didn't know it mattered.

I didn't know of muscles trained
Of stopwatch held—the race you'd won
While other parents stood and cheered
I was somewhere else detained
I was not with my son.

All the hurts you must have felt
Sat there in judgement as I knelt
With blinded eyes I'd looked beyond
The goodness you had offered me
And asked perfections one by one
Until at last I lost my son.

I am alone with just deserts
A partnership in ancient hurts
Haunted still by one prize letter
That in it's youth deserved a sweater
A "G" in blue stares back at me
Telling how it came to be.

Untreasured time so quickly flown
You and your years so soon are gone
I search to find my cupboard bare
But for the trophies you left there.

The Vigil

I miss you honey
You've only left and yet I miss you,
It's lovely here
You could be getting tan
Your sweet brown form at rest
Upon the backyard green
With the little radio
That's tied with string
Beside you.
It's quiet now, the radio
Faithful in its silent wait
For your return.

I miss the brownness of your face
Your hair and eyes
The way you smile
And the sudden way you move
About the house,
I miss telling you "goodnight"
And watching
As you close the closet door
To keep away the ghosts.

The little sign that says to
"Pick up Julie"
Lies neglected in my top desk drawer,
Still you must know that I am happy
That you are doing what you are,
I am proud that you at seventeen
Have stepped into your future
It's just that I'm not used to all this quiet.

Dating Game

It might be better not to call
To never lift the phone at all
Than offer sweet translucent hope
That tempting pathways just might open
To adventure,
Then place the unknown on a shelf
And tag him
With an ill-begotten label.

The label cannot understand
The product it defaces
It has no intellect to know
The depth or span
Of who is holding in her hand
The other-ended phone,
Who bird-like says hello-goodbye
With no one knowing who it is
Or caring
As both are lacking in adventure
The caller and the phone.

You say that you like poetry?
And music...also laughter?
Well, sir, I am these,
I am a laughing poem
With music flowing from
My fingertips.
But you did not discover this
Because too quick the phone
Went to its cradle
With neither of you wondering
Just who I was.

And, sir, I could not offer up to you
I am a poem. I'm born and bred discreet,
Some things must not be said
But only understood.
I cannot say I am a singing
Laughing poem,
A dedication to lightening
The grays that fog the world,
And should I say it
I doubt you would believe.

I'm resting easy on my shelf
I'm shocked that I am able
But truly I'd appreciate
If you'd remove the label.

A Ballad of The
Old-Time Country Dance

We were store-clothed all proper with a tan
    of ruddy hue,
We were bathed and freshly shaven with a
    whiff of perfume too
Though our hands were gnarled and calloused we had
    virile fun in store
When we went to country dances in the
    happy days of yore.

Made our way with horse and buggy with a
    duster o'er our knees
Not to keep the dust from off us but our vanity to please,
With our whale-bone whips a-cracking to a
    neighbor's near demesne
Or the new barn he was building with its unused floor
    all clean.

With numbers cut from calendars adorning their lapels
The men-folks in rotation danced that harmony might
    dwell.
The girls and women waited till some man
    asked them to dance
Then moved with grace so perfect as to capture every
    glance.

We set the fiddle scraping with the strum of a guitar
And sometimes a sweet mouth-organ like a thrush heard
    from afar,
Though some danced in lusty fashion we did not that
    fact deplore
When we danced till early morning in those virile days
    of yore.

Oh, the whinning of the fiddle and the
    slapping leather shoes
And the hearty caller shouting "Swing your partner if
    you choose,"
With a row of bashful farm hands who without
    a partner stood
Edged about the room a-standing just like
    stolid mummies would.

Oh, the raucous whine of fiddle, how it still sounds in
    my ears
Though the dancers have departed, now grown lame
    and halt with years,
May they still dance on in fancy, feeble man and
    graying maid
With the shadow caller calling "Grab your partners,
    promenade!"

by Orman L. Miller

Ad Infinitum

All things of mine that I most need to say
Are greater than their own words — thinned with use.
Lo then my dwelling, learn this better way
The Order of Law's bloodstained peace pursuit.

Sly fetters once ignored now swift-growing
Mold deep the calloused flesh long held interned,
Turned eyes, the other cheek collect their sowings
First dies the promise then the bridges burn.

Come calling please! Come enter my abode!
Awaken! Look around! Unloose your shell!
Push back those rosy curtains and behold
The endless hovered presence of my hell.

Rend, tear the veil — combust the insulation
Be born again while raging toward salvation.

September 8, 1889 — November 5, 1972

I told her
How we all
Had loved her
Through the years.

I asked
If I could
Take her to dinner,
To a show.

I sat and visited
Without end
And talked with her
About her early days.

I promised
I would take her shopping
For the bright red coat
She'd wanted for so long

All this I did
November sixth.

The following poem was written on February 14 of no
particular year by my youngest daughter and I am
including it as most of those she refers to in her poem
can also be found in the text of *Dear Mom*, and I thought
it a fitting inclusion. In fact, the girl "who just loved
kids" provided the photo for the back cover and the "girl
who painted pictures fair" is Victoria, who did the art
work for the book.

A Valentine Poem

'Twas known about a family where
The mother had eight kids
She loved them all so dearly and
Was always glad she did.

The oldest from Alaska
Built a boat so grand
Throughout the seas she'd sail it
And in between, the land.

The next, a girl, she knew her stuff
'Bout how to decorate
The boat became magenta and
The sails the gray of slate.

Another son, a craftsman fine
He made his mom a stool
With furniture he filled her house
She thought, "My boy is cool."

Next girl she painted pictures fair
Of elbows and a tummy
Of pygmies cars and kangaroos
And gave them all to Mummy.

A son again and how he played
His music filled the skies
He filled her home with lively tunes
And Mother thought him wise.

Her long-haired son who rode his bikes
He gave his Mom a chopper
He taught her how to ride it
And not one cop could stop her.

The next a girl who just loved kids
Said "Mom please have one more."
But Mom said "No, not even one"
Said girl "Then how 'bout four?"

The youngest one she danced a lot
'Twas nothing more she'd ruther
Except to write a poem to say
"You know I love you Mother."

— by Julie Hepton